Empowered 2

ACT

Maintaining The Pillars Of Patriotism

RC Williams & Julianna Ormond

*First Edition published by Lu Rose Holdings, LLC 2024
Copyright © 2024 by LuRose Holdings, LLC, RC Williams &
Julianna Ormond. All rights reserved. No part of this publication
may be reproduced, stored or transmitted in any form or by any
means, electronic, mechanical, photocopying, recording, scanning,
or otherwise without written permission from the publisher. It is
illegal to copy this book, post it to a website, or distribute it by
any other means without permission.*

RC Williams & Julianna Ormond assert the moral right to be identified as the author of this work.

About The Authors

Husband and wife team, RC Williams and Julianna Ormond, met in 2014, each with a deep passion for servant leadership. This led them to help over 200 small businesses grow through weekly entrepreneurship meetings and through the insights from their market research technology, ParAible, & their firm, **Sherloc**.

"Our God-given gifts are definitely connecting the proverbial dots," says Ormond. "It's all about people's three levels of knowing... First is, 'you know that you know.' Second is, 'you know that you don't know but can find the information.' But then there's the third, 'you don't know that you don't know, but really need to know.' This is why we created Sherloc.... Because we needed to know! So why not share the insights."

"The third one is significant," says Williams. "The 'you don't know that you don't know, but really need to know' is where you'll find the goldmines and the landmines for potential successes or failures."

Watchmen Action's focus is to connect like-minded individuals to one another, and to the tools & resources they need to collectively flip the balance of power back to We, the People.

Watchmen Action grew out of our co-founder's sense of moral obligation, as Watchmen, to share what they were learning thanks to their market research findings. This also led to the launch of their two publications, **Ripped From The Headlines**, which breaks down what the news really means, and **We Are The Watchmen Weekly**, which connects the dots between current events and scripture.

Table of Contents

1: The Power of Principles — 8
2: Building a Community of Patriots — 11
3: The Art of Effective Communication — 15
4: Strategy Over Emotion — 19
5: Know Your Foe — 22
6: The Use of Moral Pressure — 25
7: Tactical Innovation and Adaptation — 29
8: The Power of Persistence — 33
9: Securing the Future — 37
Epilogue — 39

Introduction

The Torchbearers of Tradition

In the rapidly evolving landscape of the 21st century, where the currents of change often erode the bedrock of our societal values, the call for patriotic activism rings out with renewed urgency. "Empowered 2 ACT: Maintaining The Pillars Of Patriotism," is not merely a response to this call — it is a clarion call of its own, a manifesto for those who stand on the front lines in defense of liberty, tradition, and the enduring principles that constitute the foundation of our society.

This book is crafted for grassroots Patriots who aspire to effect meaningful change, those who seek to navigate the complexities of modern activism, while remaining steadfast to the patriotic ethos that is the foundation of America.

The Founding Fathers of OUR United States of America, with their profound understanding of our heavenly Father's laws, human nature, and our need for governance, embroidered biblically based principles into the fabric of our Constitutional Republic. And it is, has always been and always will be our duty to protect the sovereignty this land is to afford us. And together, we can ACT as they did.

They championed liberty, advocated for a balanced governance that recognized the fallibility of man, and underscored the importance of individual responsibility within the framework of community, faith, and nation- building. Their vision for a nation founded upon these principles not only shaped the United States, but also offered a beacon of hope for those who valued freedom and responsibility worldwide.

Drawing inspiration from the historical precedents set by our Founding Fathers, this book aims to empower today's Patriots. It serves as both a beacon of wisdom and a strategic manual for those committed to the conservative cause. From the tea-soaked harbors of Boston, which witnessed the early stirrings of American independence, to the philosophical debates that forged the Constitution, the spirit of patriotic activism has been a pivotal force in shaping history. This spirit, characterized by a deep reverence for the lessons of the past and a prudent approach to aligning our values for the future, is what this book seeks to ignite in the hearts of today's true Patriots.

"Empowered 2 ACT" delves into the core of what it means to be in moral alignment with our Founding Fathers in an age of 'forced' change. It acknowledges the rich tapestry of conservative thought that has been woven through the annals of history, bringing it to bear on the challenges and opportunities of contemporary activism. Through the exploration of foundational principles, the book offers not just a reflection on patriotic values, but a practical guide to advocating for them in the public square.

As we journey through the pages of this guide, from articulating the timeless principles of patriotism to mastering the art of effective communication and strategic activism, we are reminded that the path we tread is one of significance and substance. This book provides a blueprint for building resilient movements, engaging with opposition constructively, and nurturing the future torchbearers of the patriotic tradition.

In every chapter, from the strategic deployment of moral pressure to the cultivation of future leaders, "Empowered 2 ACT" stands as both a testament and a toolkit. It recognizes the challenges that lie ahead while offering hope, strategies, and inspiration for those committed to the patriotic cause. At a time when the morals of conservatism are questioned yet critical, this guide reaffirms the power and relevance of these ideas.

As you embark on this journey, let this book not only serve as your guide but also as a source of inspiration. The road of patriotic activism is fraught with challenges, yet it is also ripe with opportunities for those who dare to stand firm in their convictions.

Welcome to "Empowered 2 ACT: Maintaining The Pillars Of Patriotism." Your journey begins now, and history awaits the mark you will leave on the tapestry of our shared future.

CHAPTER 1

The Power of Principles

In the heart of every meaningful movement lies a set of core principles — a foundation upon which actions are based, goals are set, and visions are built. For grassroots Patriots, these principles are not just political positions or policy preferences; they are the bedrock of a Biblical worldview that values individual liberty, respects tradition and community, champions limited government, and upholds moral responsibility. This chapter delves into the importance of these principles, guiding Patriots in how to articulate, defend, and embody them in every facet of their patriotic activism.

The Essence of Patriotic Principles

Patriotic principles stem from a deep respect for the wisdom embedded in our traditions, an understanding of the limits of human nature and government, and a steadfast belief in the freedoms and responsibilities of individuals. These values guide Patriots in navigating the

complexities of modern society, advocating for policies and practices that reflect their deep-seated beliefs.

- **Individual Liberty:** The belief in the inherent rights of individuals to life, liberty, and the pursuit of happiness forms the cornerstone of patriotic thought. It champions the freedom of individuals to make choices and live their lives as they see fit, free from unlawful government interference.

- **Family & Community Traditions:** Patriots hold a profound respect for the lessons of history and the importance of preserving cultural heritage. They emphasize the role of family, community, and faith-based institutions in nurturing character, providing support, and shaping a healthy society.

- **Moral Responsibility:** A commitment to ethical conduct, personal responsibility, and the moral foundations of law and society is central to patriotic ideology. This includes a focus on the sanctity of life, the importance of work ethic, and the need for justice and fairness.

- **Limited Government:** Rooted in the skepticism of unchecked power, this principle advocates for a government that is restricted in its scope and size, emphasizing the role of government in protecting rights and our sovereignty.

Articulating Patriotic Principles

Effectively communicating these principles is crucial in rallying support, engaging in constructive debate, and influencing public policy. Activists must be adept at explaining how conservative values offer solutions to societal issues, from economic policy to social welfare, education, and beyond.

How-To:

- **Develop Clear Messaging:** Simplify complex ideas into clear, compelling messages that resonate with the everyday experiences of individuals.

- **Use Real-World Examples:** Illustrate conservative principles through stories and examples that highlight their positive impact on individuals and communities.

- **Engage in Dialogue:** Be open to discussions, listen actively, and respond thoughtfully to questions or criticisms, using these opportunities to deepen understanding and dispel misconceptions.

Defending Patriotic Principles

In an increasingly polarized political climate, defending patriotic principles against misunderstanding and misrepresentation is a constant challenge. Patriots must be prepared to stand firm in their convictions, offering reasoned and respectful rebuttals to critiques.

How-To:

- **Stay Informed:** Keep abreast of current events, research, and policy developments related to key issues, ensuring your arguments are grounded in facts.

- **Practice Respect:** Understand the concerns and perspectives of those who disagree, addressing their points with respect, and working to find common ground where possible.

- **Highlight Successes:** Point to historical and contemporary examples where conservative policies have led to positive outcomes, reinforcing the validity of your principles.

Conclusion

The power of patriotic principles in activism cannot be overstated. By articulating, embodying, and defending these values, grassroots Patriots can engage more effectively in the public square, contributing to a vibrant, principled debate on the future of society. As this chapter concludes, it becomes evident that principles are not just abstract ideals, but practical guides that shape action, strategy, and the pursuit of a just and free society.

CHAPTER 2

Building a Community of Patriots

At the heart of any successful grassroots movement lies a robust and engaged community. For Patriots, building this community means uniting individuals who share a commitment to principles such as liberty, tradition, and individual responsibility. But how does one transform a group of individuals into a cohesive and powerful community of Patriots? This chapter explores practical strategies for building such a community, emphasizing recruitment, engagement, and the nurturing of a shared vision.

Identifying Potential Community Members

Start by identifying where potential community members might gather, both online and in the real world. Social media platforms, local community centers, churches, and patriotic events are fertile grounds for recruitment. Look for individuals expressing conservative values or dissatisfaction with the current state of affairs aligning with patriotic perspectives.

How-To:

- **Engage on Social Media:** Join conservative groups and forums. Participate in discussions and share content that resonates with patriotic values.

- **Attend Local Events:** Be present at town hall meetings, lectures, or local GOP gatherings. These are excellent opportunities to meet like-minded individuals.

- **Host Informative Sessions:** Organize events on topics of conservative interest. Use these as opportunities to educate and recruit interested individuals.

Building a Cohesive Community

Once you've identified potential members, the next step is to foster a sense of unity and purpose. Effective communication, shared goals, and mutual respect are crucial in this phase.

How-To:

- **Establish Clear Communication Channels:** Create online groups or email lists to keep everyone informed and engaged.

- **Define Shared Goals:** Early on, establish what the community aims to achieve. Whether it's influencing local politics, supporting patriotic candidates, or raising awareness on specific issues, having clear objectives unites the group.

- **Promote Mutual Respect:** Encourage open, respectful dialogue within the group. Diverse viewpoints within the patriotic spectrum should be acknowledged and valued.

Engagement and Activation

An engaged community is an active community. Regular meetings, events, and activities keep members involved and motivated. We highly recommend meeting in person but also having a video link going so those who cannot attend in person, can still be involved.

How-To:

- **Regular Meetings:** Hold regular meetings to discuss progress, plan activities, and share insights. These can be in-person or virtual. *Pro Tip: Keep these meetings on time and utilize Robert' s Rules Of Order.*

- **Organize Events:** Whether it's a rally, a seminar, or a fundraiser, organizing events gives the community a focus and brings public attention to your cause.

- **Volunteer Opportunities:** Encourage members to volunteer for patriotic candidates, causes, and organizations. This not only supports the wider movement, but also strengthens the community's bond.

Case Study: The Tea Party Movement

A prime example of effective community building within the conservative sphere is the Tea Party movement. Emerging in 2009, the movement quickly galvanized Patriots across the United States, driven by concerns over government spending, taxation, and the push for a more limited government. The Tea Party's success lay in its ability to build a decentralized network of local groups, each united by common, patriotic principles but free to pursue their individually needed objectives.

Keys to Success:

- **Decentralized Organization:** The Tea Party's strength came from its grassroots foundation, with local groups operating independently yet cohesively.

- **Effective Use of Social Media and Digital Tools:** The movement adeptly used social media to connect members, organize events, and spread its message.

- **Clear, Unifying Message:** Despite its decentralized nature, the Tea Party maintained a clear and unifying focus on fiscal conservatism, attracting a broad base of support.

Conclusion

Building a community of Patriots is both a challenge and an opportunity. It requires patience, dedication, and a strategic approach. By identifying potential members, fostering a cohesive community, keeping members engaged, and learning from successful movements like the Tea Party, Patriots can build powerful grassroots movements capable of effecting significant change. The key is to remember that the strength of a community lies not just in its numbers, but in its commitment to shared values and goals.

CHAPTER 3

The Art of Effective Communication

Communication is the lifeblood of any movement, essential not only for spreading its message, but also for rallying support, educating the public, and influencing policy. For grassroots Patriots, mastering the art of effective communication means finding the right balance between passion and reason, and between tradition and the challenges of the modern world. This chapter delves into strategies for making patriotic voices heard in a crowded and often contentious media landscape.

Crafting a Compelling Message

The foundation of effective communication is a clear, compelling message that resonates with both the core supporters and the wider public. This message should articulate conservative principles in a way that is relevant to the issues of the day.

How-To:

- **Simplify Your Message:** Break down complex issues into key points that are easily understood by people without specialized knowledge.

- **Appeal to Universal Values:** Frame your message in terms of universal values like freedom, morality, and community. This broadens its appeal.

- **Use Stories and Analogies:** People relate to stories more than abstract concepts. Use real-life examples to illustrate your points.

Utilizing Multiple Platforms

In the digital age, effective communication requires a presence across multiple platforms. Traditional media, social media, blogs, podcasts, and direct mail campaigns all play a role in disseminating your message.

How-To:

- **Develop a Social Media Strategy:** Identify which platforms (e.g., Twitter, Facebook, Instagram) are most popular with your target audience and focus your efforts there.

- **Create a Blog or Website:** A central hub where people can learn more about your cause, read your latest news, and find out how to get involved.

- **Engage with Traditional Media:** Write op-eds, press releases, and letters to the editor for local and national newspapers.

Engaging with the Public

Public engagement goes beyond broadcasting a message; it involves listening, responding, and adapting. Engaging effectively with the public means being present in the community, at events, and in forums where public opinion is shaped.

How-To:

- **Host and Participate in Events:** Whether virtual or in-person, events are a great way to engage directly with supporters and skeptics alike. *Pro Tip: Keep these meetings on time and utilize Robert's Rules Of Order.*

- **Conduct Q&A Sessions:** Regular Q&A sessions, either online or in community meetings, can help address concerns and dispel myths.

- **Be Responsive on Social Media:** Engage with followers by responding to comments and messages. This builds a sense of community and shows that you value their input.

Navigating Controversy

In today's polarized environment, conservative messages often attract controversy. Handling this requires tact and a firm commitment to your principles.

How-To:

- **Stay Informed:** Be well-versed in the issues you're discussing. This prepares you to respond confidently to criticism.

- **Maintain Civility:** Always engage respectfully, even (and especially) when others do not.

- **Use Controversy to Educate:** Use contentious issues as opportunities to clarify your stance and educate people on conservative principles.

Case Study: The Federalist Society

The Federalist Society for Law and Public Policy Studies offers an exemplary model of effective communication within conservative circles. Founded in 1982, it has grown to become a pivotal force in American legal thought and policy, largely due to its adept use of communication strategies.

Keys to Success:

- **Focused Message:** The Federalist Society has consistently centered its communications on promoting an originalist interpretation of the U.S.
  Constitution, appealing to both legal scholars and the general public.

- **Strategic Use of Platforms:** By organizing events, publishing scholarly articles, and engaging in public discourse, the Society has effectively spread its message across multiple channels.

- **Engagement with Critics:** The Federalist Society has not shied away from engaging with its critics, often hosting debates and discussions that highlight the strength of its arguments.

Conclusion

Effective communication is not just about speaking; it's about being heard. For grassroots conservatives, it involves crafting a message that resonates, utilizing multiple platforms to reach a broad audience, engaging in meaningful dialogue with the public, and navigating controversy with grace and conviction. By following these strategies, conservatives can ensure their message not only reaches but also inspires and mobilizes those who hear it.

CHAPTER 4

Strategy Over Emotion

In the realm of patriotic activism, passion and emotion are powerful motivators. They drive individuals to take action, speak out, and stand firm in their beliefs. However, for a movement to achieve lasting impact and navigate the complexities of the political landscape, *strategy* must guide the way. This chapter emphasizes the importance of strategic planning, goal setting, and the disciplined pursuit of objectives, ensuring that emotional energy is channeled effectively into actions that advance patriotic principles.

The Role of Strategy in Activism

A well-defined strategy serves as a roadmap for Patriots, outlining clear paths toward achieving specific goals. It ensures that resources— time, energy, and funds— are allocated efficiently, and it helps movements maintain focus amid the ever-shifting dynamics of public opinion and political debate.

How-To:

- **Set Clear, Achievable Goals:** Define what success looks like for your movement, whether it's influencing policy, electing patriotic candidates, or changing public opinion on key issues. Ensure goals are **specific, measurable, achievable, relevant, and time-bound** (SMART).

- **Analyze the Landscape:** Understand the political, social, and cultural context in which you operate. Identify allies and opponents, assess public sentiment, and recognize opportunities and threats.

- **Develop a Tactical Plan:** Break down your goals into actionable steps. Determine which tactics will be most effective in your context, from grassroots organizing and social media campaigns to lobbying and public demonstrations.

Balancing Emotion and Strategy

While strategy should lead, the role of emotion in motivating and energizing activists cannot be understated. The challenge lies in balancing the two, ensuring that emotional appeals are grounded in strategic objectives.

How-To:

- **Harness Emotion Effectively:** Use emotional stories and messaging to connect with people on a personal level, but always tie these back to your strategic goals.

- **Avoid Reactive Tactics:** In response to opposition actions or current events, assess the situation through the lens of your strategy before acting. This helps prevent knee-jerk reactions that may be off- mission.

- **Train and Educate Activists:** Equip your members with the knowledge and skills they need to understand and implement your strategy, helping them channel their passion into effective action.

Implementing and Adapting Your Strategy

The only constant in activism is change. As such, even the best-laid plans must be subject to review and adaptation.

How-To:

- **Monitor Progress and Impact:** Regularly review your goals and the effectiveness of your tactics. Use both qualitative and quantitative measures to assess progress.

- **Be Prepared to Pivot:** If certain strategies aren't working or if the political landscape shifts, be willing to adjust your approach. Flexibility can be a key asset in responding to new challenges.

- **Foster a Culture of Learning:** Encourage your team to learn from both successes and failures. Create a space where constructive feedback is welcomed and used to strengthen future efforts.

Conclusion

Strategic planning does not dampen the passion that fuels patriotic activism; rather, it channels that passion into focused, effective efforts that can achieve real change. By prioritizing strategy over emotion, Patriots can ensure their movement not only resonates with people on an emotional level, but also moves steadily toward its goals. This chapter has laid out the tools and approaches necessary to create a disciplined, strategic foundation for patriotic activism, empowering grassroots movements to navigate the complexities of the political arena with confidence and precision.

CHAPTER 5

Know Your Foe

In the landscape of patriotic activism, understanding your opposition is as crucial as knowing your own stance. For grassroots Patriots, this means going beyond surface-level disagreements to grasp the underlying philosophies, strategies, and goals of those with opposing viewpoints. This chapter offers guidance on respectfully engaging with and effectively countering the arguments and tactics of opposition groups, all while maintaining the integrity and principles of patriotic activism.

The Importance of Understanding Your Opposition

Grasping the motivations and beliefs of those who oppose patriotic values can illuminate areas of common ground and highlight key differences. It aids in preparing more effective arguments, anticipates challenges, and fosters a more respectful and productive public discourse.

How-To:

- **Conduct Thorough Research:** Dive into the literature, speeches, and publications of opposing groups to understand their arguments and objectives.

- **Attend Their Events:** When possible, attend debates, lectures, and public forums hosted by or featuring those with opposing views. Listening firsthand can provide valuable insights.

- **Engage in Civil Dialogue:** Seek opportunities for conversation with individuals who hold different views. These interactions can reveal the nuances of oppositional thought and the reasons behind certain beliefs.

Crafting Effective Counterstrategies

With a solid understanding of your opposition, you can develop nuanced counterstrategies that address the core of their arguments, appeal to undecided audiences, and reinforce the strengths of patriotic principles.

How-To:

- **Highlight Logical and Factual Inconsistencies:** Use your knowledge to respectfully challenge inaccuracies or logical flaws in opposing arguments.

- **Emphasize Shared Values:** Where possible, bridge divides by highlighting values and goals you have in common with your opposition, and then clarify how patriotic approaches better serve those shared interests.

- **Prepare for Common Tactics:** Anticipate and prepare for the tactics often used by opposition groups, whether it appeals to emotion, misrepresentation of facts, or other strategies.

Balancing Firmness with Integrity

Engaging with the opposition is not about winning every argument, but about advancing the conversation in a way that maintains integrity. This approach not only upholds the dignity of political discourse but also attracts those on the fence by demonstrating the strength and reasonableness of conservative positions.

How-To:

- **Maintain a Respectful Tone:** Even in disagreement, respect for the person and their right to hold a different opinion is paramount. Avoid ad hominem attacks or dismissive language.

- **Acknowledge Valid Points:** Recognizing the strengths or valid concerns in opposing arguments can demonstrate open-mindedness and build credibility.

- **Focus on Patriotic Facts:** Keep discussions centered on information and the foundational principles of patriotism to avoid getting sidetracked by emotional or irrelevant points.

Conclusion

Understanding and engaging with your opposition is not an acknowledgment of their correctness but a strategic approach that strengthens your advocacy. It allows for the development of more refined, effective strategies that can withstand criticism and appeal to a broader audience. By approaching opposition with a mindset geared towards learning and respect, grassroots Patriots can enhance their effectiveness, promote civil discourse, and underscore the integrity of their cause. This chapter has laid out the framework for not only knowing your opposition but engaging with them in ways that further the principles and goals of patriotic activism.

CHAPTER 6

The Use of Moral Pressure

In the pursuit of social and political change, moral pressure is a powerful tool. It leverages the ethical and moral values of the broader community to persuade, influence public opinion, and prompt action. For Patriots, who often ground their principles in long-standing traditions and ethical norms, the strategic use of moral pressure can be particularly effective. This chapter explores how grassroots conservatives can harness moral arguments to advance their cause, shape public discourse, and effect policy changes.

Understanding Moral Pressure

Moral pressure involves invoking shared values and ethical standards to challenge or support specific actions, policies, or societal norms. It's a call to conscience that urges individuals, communities, and leaders to act in alignment with what is broadly considered morally right or just.

How-To:

- **Identify Core Values:** Start by clearly defining the moral and ethical values central to your cause. These might include personal responsibility, respect for life, the importance of family, and the preservation of freedom.

- **Connect Values to Issues:** Draw clear connections between these values and the issues you're addressing. Make it evident how your stance is rooted in deeply held moral beliefs.

Crafting Moral Arguments

Effective moral arguments are clear, compelling, and resonate with a broad audience. They appeal to the sense of right and wrong ingrained in human consciousness.

How-To:

- **Use Clear, Accessible Language:** Avoid jargon or overly complex language that might alienate your audience.

- **Incorporate Stories and Testimonials:** Personal stories and testimonials can powerfully illustrate moral points, making abstract principles tangible and relatable.

- **Highlight Common Ground:** Emphasize values and ethical principles that are widely shared, even with those who might initially disagree with your position.

Mobilizing Public Opinion

Moral pressure can shift public opinion by framing issues in terms of widely accepted ethical principles. This can lead to a broader base of support, influencing policymakers and the direction of public policy.

How-To:

- **Public Campaigns:** Use public speaking opportunities, social media, and traditional media to disseminate your message.

- **Engage with Community Leaders:** Seek the support of respected community leaders who can lend their voice and influence to your cause.

- **Organize Peaceful Demonstrations:** Demonstrations and rallies can visibly showcase public support for your moral stance.

Responding to Opposition

When employing moral pressure, anticipate and prepare for opposition. The key is to respond in a way that reinforces your ethical stance and opens the door to constructive dialogue.

How-To:

- **Maintain Respectful Engagement:** Always engage respectfully, even in the face of hostility. This strengthens the moral integrity of your position.

- **Fact-Check and Counter:** Be prepared to fact-check and politely correct misinformation or misinterpretations of your stance.

- **Seek Dialogue, Not Confrontation:** Aim for constructive dialogue that can lead to mutual understanding, even if agreement isn't immediately possible - you never know who is watching or listening.

Case Study: The Pro-Life Movement

A compelling example of the effective use of moral pressure is the pro-life movement. Regardless of individual positions on this issue, it's undeniable that the pro-life movement has significantly influenced public discourse, policy, and legislation in the United States.

Keys to Success:

- **Clear Moral Argument:** The pro-life movement has been effective in framing its stance as a defense of the right to life, a fundamental moral and ethical principle.

- **Broad Coalition Building:** By appealing to a wide array of ethical beliefs and backgrounds, the movement has built a diverse coalition.

- **Persistent Public Engagement:** Through marches, educational campaigns, and public speaking, the movement has kept the issue at the forefront of public consciousness.

Conclusion

The use of moral pressure is a testament to the power of ethical and moral persuasion. For Patriots, it offers a pathway to engage the public, influence policy, and advocate for change based on deeply held values. By crafting compelling moral arguments, mobilizing public opinion, and engaging respectfully with opposition, conservatives can effectively harness this tool in their efforts to shape the future.

CHAPTER 7

Tactical Innovation and Adaptation

In the dynamic landscape of political and social activism, the ability to innovate and adapt tactically is crucial for maintaining momentum and achieving objectives. For grassroots Patriots, this means being flexible in approach while steadfast in principles. This chapter explores strategies for fostering innovation in tactics and adapting to changing circumstances, ensuring that patriotic movements remain resilient and effective.

Embracing Tactical Innovation

Innovation in tactics involves exploring new methods, technologies, and approaches to advocacy and engagement. It's about thinking creatively to overcome challenges and capitalize on opportunities.

How-To:

- **Encourage Creativity:** Create an environment within your organization or movement where new ideas are welcomed and considered. Regular brainstorming sessions can spark innovative tactics.

- **Stay Informed on Technologies:** The digital landscape is always evolving. Stay informed about new technologies and platforms that can enhance your communication, organization, and outreach efforts.

- **Learn from Other Movements:** Observe and learn from the tactics of other political and social movements, even those with differing ideologies. There's much to learn from their successes and failures.

Adapting to Changing Circumstances

The ability to adapt is key to navigating the unpredictable nature of grassroots activism. Adaptation might mean altering tactics in response to political shifts, public sentiment, or the actions of opposition groups.

How-To:

- **Monitor the Political and Social Climate:** Keep a close eye on changes in the political landscape and public opinion. This will help you anticipate shifts that could impact your strategy.

- **Flexible Planning:** While having a clear strategy is essential, be prepared to modify your plans as circumstances change. Set short-term goals that can be adjusted as needed.

- **Rapid Response Capability:** Develop the ability to respond quickly to unexpected events or opportunities. This could mean having a team ready to mobilize at short notice or using digital platforms to react swiftly to developments.

Case Study: The Use of Social Media in Patriotic Activism

The conservative movement has seen significant success in utilizing social media platforms to innovate tactics and adapt to the changing landscape of public discourse. By leveraging social media, conservatives have bypassed traditional media gatekeepers to reach a wider audience, mobilize support, and drive narratives.

Keys to Success:

- **Direct Engagement:** Social media allows for direct communication with supporters and the broader public, enabling rapid dissemination of information and mobilization of grassroots efforts.

- **Viral Content Creation:** Innovative use of memes, videos, and other shareable content has allowed conservative messages to spread widely and quickly.

- **Adaptation to Platform Algorithms:** Successful patriotic activists have learned to adapt their messaging and content strategies to maximize visibility and engagement within the constraints of social media algorithms.

Overcoming Resistance to Change

Innovation and adaptation can sometimes be met with resistance within movements, especially those with deeply held traditions and established ways of operating. Having said that, this is not an excuse to find yourself and your organization in this situation. Remember, *change* is the only thing that is consistent in activism.

How-To:

- **Communicate the Benefits:** Clearly articulate how new tactics and flexibility can lead to greater success and further the movement's goals.

- **Lead by Example:** Demonstrate the effectiveness of new approaches through test projects, small groups, or case studies.

- **Provide Training and Support:** Offer resources and training to help members become comfortable with new technologies and tactics.

Conclusion

Tactical innovation and adaptation are not about abandoning core principles but about finding new and effective ways to advocate for those patriotic principles in a constantly changing world. By embracing creativity, staying informed, learning from both successes and failures, and being prepared to pivot when necessary, grassroots Patriots can enhance their impact and navigate the challenges of modern activism. The use of social media in conservative activism demonstrates the power of innovative and adaptable tactics in reaching and mobilizing support in the digital age.

CHAPTER 8

The Power of Persistence

Persistence is the fuel that keeps the engine of patriotic activism running, especially in the face of challenges and setbacks. For grassroots Patriots, the journey toward achieving significant social and political change is often a marathon, not a sprint. This chapter focuses on the importance of perseverance, strategies for maintaining long-term commitment, and the ways in which sustained efforts can lead to breakthroughs and successes.

Understanding the Value of Persistence

Persistence in activism means consistently pushing forward towards your goals, despite obstacles or discouragement. It's about maintaining focus and energy over the long haul, understanding that most significant achievements require time, effort, and unwavering dedication.

How-To:

- **Set Realistic Expectations:** Understand that change usually happens gradually. Setting realistic expectations helps prevent burnout and disillusionment.

- **Celebrate Small Wins:** Recognize and celebrate the small victories along the way. This can boost morale and remind everyone involved of the progress being made.

- **Learn from Setbacks:** Instead of being discouraged by setbacks, view them as learning opportunities. Analyze what went wrong and how you can adapt your strategies moving forward.

Cultivating Resilience

Resilience is the ability to recover from difficulties and continue moving forward. It's a critical trait for activists, who often face opposition and challenges that can test their commitment and resolve.

How-To:

- **Build a Supportive Community:** Surround yourself with like-minded individuals who share your commitment. A supportive community can provide encouragement and motivation during tough times.

- **Maintain Balance:** Avoid burnout by ensuring that you're not dedicating all your time and energy to activism. Balance your efforts with activities that rejuvenate you physically, mentally, and spiritually.

- **Stay Focused on the Mission:** Remind yourself and your team of the bigger picture and the reasons why you're committed to your cause. This can help maintain motivation when the going gets tough.

Case Study: The Conservative Legal Movement

One of the most illustrative examples of the power of persistence in patriotic activism is the conservative legal movement in the United States. Over the course of several decades, this movement worked systematically to shift the judiciary and legal thought towards originalism and conservative principles.

Keys to Success:

- **Long-Term Vision:** The movement set long-term goals, understanding that changing the judiciary would take time.

- **Strategic Persistence:** Through persistent efforts, including education, advocacy, and strategic litigation, the movement gradually increased its influence.

- **Adapting Tactics:** While remaining committed to its core goals, the movement adapted its tactics as needed, responding to the changing legal and political landscape.

Navigating the Challenges of Persistence

Sustaining effort over the long term is challenging. Patriotic activists may face burnout, discouragement, and external pressures to give up.

How-To:

- **Take Care Of Yourself:** Encourage activists to take care of their physical and mental health. A movement is only as strong as its members.

- **Seek External Support:** Look for alliances and support from other groups or individuals who share your goals. External validation and support can provide a crucial boost.

- **Reevaluate and Adjust Strategies:** Be open to changing tactics and strategies as circumstances evolve. This can help keep the movement to be dynamic and responsive.

Conclusion

Persistence is a critical component of successful activism. For grassroots Patriots, the journey toward achieving their goals is often filled with obstacles and opposition. However, by setting realistic expectations, celebrating small victories, building resilience, and staying adaptable, activists can maintain their commitment and drive over the long haul.

The conservative legal movement serves as a powerful example of what can be achieved with persistent effort and strategic thinking. As activists navigate the challenges of sustained advocacy, focusing on the bigger picture and the underlying reasons for their commitment can help keep the flame of persistence burning bright.

CHAPTER 9

Securing the Future

The final chapter of our journey into grassroots activism is not just a summary of strategies and tactics, but a forward-looking vision toward securing a future that aligns with patriotic principles and values.

The longevity and vitality of the patriotic movement depend on its ability to adapt, grow, and most importantly, engage future generations in the cause. This chapter outlines the importance of education, mentorship, and the development of conservative leadership as crucial steps in ensuring that the torch of patriotic values is passed on and remains bright in the years to come.

Engaging the Younger Generations

The future of patriotism lies in the hands of the youth. Engaging with younger generations, therefore, is essential. This engagement involves understanding their concerns, speaking their language, and demonstrating how patriotic principles address the issues they care about most.

How-To:

- **Educational Initiatives:** Support and develop educational programs that provide young people with a balanced understanding of patriotic principles, history, and their application to contemporary issues.

- **Social Media Engagement:** Utilize platforms where younger audiences spend their time. Content should be engaging, informative, and crafted in a way that resonates with the younger generations' values and interests.

- **Youth Leadership Programs:** Create opportunities for young Patriots to develop their leadership skills, understand the political process, and become active participants in the movement.

Building a Culture of Mentorship

Mentorship is a powerful tool for personal and professional development. By fostering a culture of mentorship within the patriotic movement, experienced activists can guide and nurture the next generation of leaders.

How-To:

- **Establish Mentorship Programs:** Pair young conservatives with experienced mentors who can offer guidance, support, and insight into navigating the complexities of activism and leadership.

- **Encourage Intergenerational Dialogue:** Organize forums and discussions that allow for the exchange of ideas and experiences between older and younger conservatives, fostering mutual respect and learning.

Developing Patriotic Leadership

The sustainability of the patriotic movement depends on a steady stream of informed, articulate, and principled leaders. Developing such leaders requires a commitment to education, ethical conduct, and the cultivation of strategic thinking and effective communication skills.

How-To:

- **Leadership Training Workshops:** Offer workshops and seminars focused on developing key leadership skills, including public speaking, strategic planning, and organizational management.

- **Promote Ethical Leadership:** Emphasize the importance of integrity, humility, and service in leadership, aligning personal conduct with conservative principles.

- **Support Aspiring, Like-Minded Politicians:** Provide resources, training, and support for conservatives interested in running for public office, ensuring they are well-equipped to campaign effectively and govern according to conservative values.

Conclusion

As we look towards the future, the patriotic movement stands at a crossroads. The choices made today will shape not only the immediate future, but the legacy of *patriotism* for generations to come. By investing in the education and engagement of young people, fostering a culture of mentorship, and developing strong, principled leaders, the movement can ensure its principles continue to influence society and policy. This chapter, and indeed this book, serves as a call to action for all Patriots to play an active role in securing a future that reflects the values we hold dear.

The journey of patriotic activism is long and filled with challenges, but with commitment, strategy, and unity, our movement can thrive, preserving the ideals of liberty, tradition, and individual responsibility for the future.

Epilogue

It's **YOUR** *Time For Action*

As we turn the final page of this guide, it's important to remember that the journey of grassroots patriotic activism is an ongoing one. The strategies, principles, and examples discussed in the preceding chapters are not just a blueprint for action, but a call to a deeper commitment to the values and ideals that define our movement. This journey is characterized by the enduring belief in individual liberty, respect for tradition, the rule of law, and the importance of community and family.

The path of patriotic activism is fraught with challenges, yet it is also paved with the potential for profound impact and lasting change. The stories of persistence, innovation, and principled action shared in this book are not the end, but a beginning. They are a testament to what can be achieved when dedicated individuals come together for a cause greater than themselves.

Looking Forward

As we look to the future, the landscape of political and social activism will undoubtedly continue to evolve. New challenges will emerge, and with them, the need for new strategies and adaptations.

However, the core principles that underpin patriotic activism will remain unchanged. These timeless values will continue to serve as a compass, guiding our movement through whatever storms may come.

The task ahead is monumental, and the road is long. Yet, the history of the patriotic movement is filled with examples of remarkable achievements born from commitment, courage, and conviction. Each victory, no matter how small, is a step toward a future where patriotic values and principles play a vital role in shaping society.

A Call to Action

This book is, above all, a call to *action*. It is an invitation to engage, to speak out, and to stand up for the principles you believe in. The success of our patriotic movement depends not on the few but on the many. It relies on the passion, intelligence, and dedication of grassroots Patriots who are willing to put in the work required to make a difference by leading.

You have the tools, the knowledge, and the examples of those who have walked this path before you. Now, it is up to you to take the next step. Whether it's organizing your local community, engaging in thoughtful debate, or simply living out your principles in your daily life, every action counts.

In Closing

Let this book not just be a resource, but a source of inspiration. Let it remind you that your voice matters, your efforts are valuable, and your commitment can lead to real change. The patriotic movement is a tapestry woven from the actions of individuals who dared to believe that their contributions could create a brighter future.

As you close this book, remember that the end of one chapter, is the beginning of another. The story of patriotic activism is still being written, and you have a role to play in it. Let us move forward with resolve and hope, united by our shared values and driven by our vision for a better world.

Together, we can ensure that our principles of patriotism continue to light the way toward a future marked by freedom, prosperity, and a blessed hope for all.

Resources: Tools In The Toolbox

To delve deeper into the themes and principles discussed in "Empowered 2 ACT: Maintaining The Pillars Of Patriotism," a variety of resources can enrich your understanding and engagement with conservative values and strategies.

From the Authors

- Our Power Is We, The People:
  Watchmen Action - WatchmenAction.org

- Equipping The Church To Engage the Culture By Connecting The Dots Between Current Events & Scripture: We Are The Watchmen Weekly - WeAreTheWatchmen.org

- Dissecting Today's News & Telling You What It All Means: Ripped From the Headlines - SherlocExposes.com

Historical Documents

- **The Federalist Papers:** A collection of 85 articles and essays written by Alexander Hamilton, James Madison, and John Jay promoting the ratification of the United States Constitution.

- **"Common Sense" by Thomas Paine:** A pivotal pamphlet that argued for American independence from Britain and the creation of a republic.

- **"Declaration of Independence":** The foundational document of the United States, outlining the principles of freedom and self-governance.

- **"Speeches and Letters of Abraham Lincoln, 1832- 1865":** A collection of writings from one of America's most revered Presidents, offering insights into his conservative views on liberty, union, and governance.

- **Gen. Dwight D. Eisenhower's farewell address, January 17, 1961:** A seminal resource for conservative principles, particularly known for its prescient warning about the "military-industrial complex."

Made in the USA
Middletown, DE
22 August 2024